SELECT SERIES

Sauces & Marinades

by JEAN PARÉ

Company's Coming

COOKBOOKS

Sauces & Marinades

First printing May 1997

Canadian Cataloguing in Publication Data

Paré, Jean

     Sauces & marinades

Includes index.
Published also in French under title: Sauces et marinades.
ISBN 1-896891-02-0

     1. Sauces. 2. Marinades. I. Title. II. Title: Sauces & marinades.

TX819.A1P368 1997   641.8'14   C97-900039-4

Published simultaneously in
Canada and the United States of America by
The Recipe Factory Inc.
in conjunction with
Company's Coming Publishing Limited
2311 - 96 Street
Edmonton, Alberta, Canada T6N 1G3
Tel: 403 • 450-6223
Fax: 403 • 450-1857

Company's Coming
COOKBOOKS®

Sauces & Marinades was created thanks to the dedicated efforts of the people and organizations listed below.

COMPANY'S COMING PUBLISHING LIMITED

Author	Jean Paré
President	Grant Lovig
Production Manager	Kathy Knowles
Production Coordinator	Derrick Sorochan
Design	Nora Cserny
Typesetting	Marlene Crosbie
	Debbie Dixon

THE RECIPE FACTORY INC.

Managing Editor	Nora Prokop
Test Kitchen Supervisor	Lynda Elsenheimer
Assistant Editor	Stephanie With
Photographer	Stephe Tate Photo
Food Stylist	Stephanie With
Prop Stylist	Gabriele McEleney

Our special thanks to the following businesses for providing extensive props for photography.

Chintz & Company
Creations By Design
Enchanted Kitchen
La Cache
Le Gnome
Stokes
The Bay Housewares Dept.

Color separations, printing, and binding by Friesens, Altona, Manitoba, Canada
Printed in Canada

FRONT COVER
Clockwise from top right:
Christmas Pudding Sauce, page 33
Parsley Sauce, page 54
Cranberry Applesauce, page 43

Table of Contents

The Jean Paré Story

Jean Paré grew up understanding that the combination of family, friends and home cooking is the essence of a good life. From her mother she learned to appreciate good cooking, while her father praised even her earliest attempts. When she left home she took with her many acquired family recipes, her love of cooking and her intriguing desire to read recipe books like novels!

In 1963, when her four children had all reached school age, Jean volunteered to cater to the 50th anniversary of the Vermilion School of Agriculture, now Lakeland College. Working out of her home, Jean prepared a dinner for over 1000 people which launched a flourishing catering operation that continued for over eighteen years. During that time she was provided with countless opportunities to test new ideas with immediate feedback—resulting in empty plates and contented customers! Whether preparing cocktail sandwiches for a house party or serving a hot meal for 1500 people, Jean Paré earned a reputation for good food, courteous service and reasonable prices.

"Why don't you write a cookbook?" Time and again, as requests for her recipes mounted, Jean was asked that question. Jean's response was to team up with her son, Grant Lovig, in the fall of 1980 to form Company's Coming Publishing Limited. April 14, 1981, marked the debut of "150 DELICIOUS SQUARES", the first Company's Coming cookbook in what soon would become Canada's most popular cookbook series. By 1995, sales had surpassed ten million cookbooks.

Jean Paré's operation has grown from the early days of working out of a spare bedroom in her home to operating a large and fully equipped test kitchen in Vermilion, Alberta, near the home she and her husband Larry built. Full-time staff has grown steadily to include marketing personnel located in major cities across Canada plus selected U.S. markets. Home Office is located in Edmonton, Alberta where distribution, accounting and administration functions are headquartered in the company's own 20,000 square foot facility. Growth continues with the recent addition of the Recipe Factory, a 2700 square foot test kitchen and photography studio located in Edmonton.

Company's Coming cookbooks are now distributed throughout Canada and the United States plus numerous overseas markets, all under the guidance of Jean's daughter, Gail Lovig. The series is published in English and French, plus a Spanish language edition is available in Mexico. Soon the familiar and trusted Company's Coming style of recipes will be available in a variety of formats in addition to the bestselling soft cover series.

Jean Paré's approach to cooking has always called for quick and easy recipes using everyday ingredients. She continues to gain new supporters by adhering to what she calls "the golden rule of cooking": never share a recipe you wouldn't use yourself. It's an approach that works—*ten million times over!*

Foreword

Sauces and marinades are often the unsung heroes of a truly great meal. They have that impressive ability to turn something like a simple chicken breast into an extraordinary Chicken Alfredo, or an economy cut of beef into an exotic Teriyaki Beef stir fry! When it's time for dessert, few will say no to a tantalizing chocolate sauce, carefully drizzled over a scoop of ice cream.

Sauces are, for the most part, easily adaptable to whatever flavors you are considering. Increase, decrease, or even replace the seasonings listed in the recipe for something of your own. Try using fresh instead of dried herbs (the ratio is $\frac{1}{2}$ tsp. or 2 mL dried herbs = 1 tbsp. or 15 mL of fresh). If you are concerned with sodium intake, reduce salt or remove it entirely and adjust your seasonings to taste. Fat content can also be lowered by substituting skim milk in place of 2%, whole milk or cream, and vegetable or olive oil is a good replacement for butter. Keep in mind however that the recipes in this book were tested using the ingredients listed, and your results may vary somewhat if you decide to use substitute ingredients.

Marinades are primarily used to tenderize tougher cuts of meat, but they also serve the purpose of introducing flavor directly into your food. When marinating, use a glass, ceramic or stainless-steel container, cover and place in the refrigerator. Because marinades tend to contain acidic ingredients like vinegar, it's important you never use a container made from aluminum.

Marinades can also make a great sauce. Just remember that after you have marinated your food, you will need to bring the leftover marinade to a boil first before thickening and serving.

Sauces & Marinades offers up a collection of proven recipes to complement any meal. Need a quick pasta supper? Try Marinara Sauce, page 64. Dress up broccoli with Mock Hollandaise, page 53, or give your grilled salmon some real zest with a tasty Dill Sauce, page 18. It's so easy to make a good meal great when you have the perfect sauce or marinade. With over 120 recipes to choose from, you are certain to find just what you need!

Summer or winter, everyone loves the unique flavor of a barbecued dish, whether grilled outdoors or roasted in your oven. Make your meal preparation quick and easy with these delicious barbecue and basting sauces. Barbecue sauces are most often tomato or soy sauce based, and recipes can range from sweet to smoky to spicy-hot—perfect for basting beef, pork, chicken, fish or vegetables.

TERIYAKI SAUCE

Brush on salmon steaks, chicken pieces or beef steaks.

Soy sauce	1½ tbsp.	25 mL
Brown sugar, packed	1 tbsp.	15 mL
Cooking oil	½ tsp.	2 mL
Ground ginger	1/16 tsp.	0.5 mL
Garlic powder, pinch		

Mix all 5 ingredients in small bowl. Makes 2 tbsp. (30 mL).

Pictured on page 7.

ORIENTAL SAUCE

Brush over partially cooked chicken wings. Continue to cook wings and brush with sauce. Glazes nicely.

Soy sauce	¼ cup	60 mL
Brown sugar, packed	2 tbsp.	30 mL
Onion powder	⅛ tsp.	0.5 mL
Garlic powder	⅛ tsp.	0.5 mL
Ground ginger	⅛ tsp.	0.5 mL

Mix all 5 ingredients in small bowl. Makes ⅓ cup (75 mL).

Teriyaki Sauce, page 6

BARBECUE SAUCE

This dark reddish sauce has a mild tang. Very simple and basic.

Butter or hard margarine	1 tbsp.	15 mL
Chopped onion	½ cup	125 mL
Ketchup	1 cup	250 mL
White vinegar	⅓ cup	75 mL
Water	⅓ cup	75 mL
Brown sugar, packed	3 tbsp.	50 mL
Worcestershire sauce	1 tsp.	5 mL
Prepared mustard	1 tsp.	5 mL

Melt butter in saucepan. Add onion. Sauté until soft.

Add remaining ingredients. Simmer about 20 minutes, stirring occasionally, until sauce thickens. Makes 1¼ cups (300 mL).

EASY BARBECUE SAUCE

Quick to make this from the contents off the shelf.

Water	1 cup	250 mL
Ketchup	1 cup	250 mL
Envelope dry onion soup mix	1 × 1½ oz.	1 × 42 g
Worcestershire sauce	1 tbsp.	15 mL
Ground oregano	1 tsp.	5 mL
Garlic powder	¼ tsp.	1 mL
Dried sweet basil	¼ tsp.	1 mL
Lemon juice, fresh or bottled	2 tsp.	10 mL

Measure all 8 ingredients into saucepan. Stir. Place over medium heat. Stir often until sauce boils. Simmer, uncovered, for about 10 minutes. Stir often. Makes about 1⅓ cups (325 mL).

BARBECUE SAUCE

Always fun to make from scratch. Simple but with a few more ingredients than some.

Butter or hard margarine	1 tbsp.	15 mL
Very finely chopped onion	1/3 cup	75 mL
Very finely chopped celery	1/3 cup	75 mL
Garlic clove, minced	1	1
Tomato sauce	2 × 7 1/2 oz.	2 × 213 mL
Brown sugar, packed	2 tbsp.	30 mL
Worcestershire sauce	1 tbsp.	15 mL
Red wine vinegar	1/4 cup	60 mL
Dry mustard powder	1 tbsp.	15 mL
Bay leaf	1	1
Prepared orange juice	1/2 cup	125 mL
Hot pepper sauce	1/4 tsp.	1 mL

Melt butter in frying pan. Add onion, celery, and garlic. Sauté until soft.

Add next 8 ingredients. Stir. Bring to a boil. Simmer, uncovered, for 10 minutes, stirring occasionally. Discard bay leaf. Makes 2 1/2 cups (625 mL).

Pictured below.

FRANKFURTER SAUCE

Cut cooked wieners into 1 inch (2.5 cm) pieces. Pour sauce over or dip pieces in using toothpicks.

Chili sauce	½ cup	125 mL
Brown sugar, packed	2 tbsp.	30 mL
White vinegar	2 tbsp.	30 mL
Worcestershire sauce	¼ tsp.	1 mL
Onion powder	¼ tsp.	1 mL

Mix all 5 ingredients in small bowl. Makes ¾ cup (175 mL).

GARLIC SAUCE

Makes a good dark glaze for spareribs or meatballs.

Brown sugar, packed	1 cup	250 mL
Cornstarch	2 tbsp.	30 mL
Garlic powder (or 2 cloves, minced)	½ tsp.	2 mL
Water	1 cup	250 mL
Soy sauce	3 tbsp.	50 mL

Mix all 5 ingredients in small saucepan. Heat and stir until sauce boils and thickens. Makes 1⅓ cups (325 mL).

PARÉ
pointer

If you shout around

trees you will have a

petrified forest.

BUSH FIRE STEAK SAUCE

Make this as hot as you want. Serve with steaks.

Ketchup	⅓ cup	75 mL
Worcestershire sauce	1½ tsp.	7 mL
Lemon juice, fresh or bottled	2 tbsp.	30 mL
Dry mustard powder	1 tsp.	5 mL
Paprika	½ tsp.	2 mL
Pepper	¼ tsp.	1 mL
Hot pepper sauce	¼-½ tsp.	1-2 mL
Butter or hard margarine	½ cup	125 mL

Combine all 8 ingredients in saucepan. Place on edge of barbecue grill or over low heat on stove. Heat and stir to melt butter. Makes 1 cup (250 mL).

Pictured on this page.

SMOKEY SAUCE

Brush over chicken wings before baking. Continue to brush and bake until cooked.

Granulated sugar	1½ tbsp.	25 mL
Salt	1 tsp.	5 mL
Pepper	⅛ tsp.	0.5 mL
Cornstarch	½ tsp.	2 mL
Onion powder	¼ tsp.	1 mL
Ketchup	3 tbsp.	50 mL
White vinegar	1 tbsp.	15 mL
Worcestershire sauce	1½ tsp.	7 mL
Liquid smoke	⅛ tsp.	0.5 mL

Mix first 5 ingredients in small bowl.

Add remaining 4 ingredients. Stir well. Makes ⅓ cup (75 mL).

HONEY MUSTARD SAUCE

Brush this on ham for barbecuing or baking.

Brown sugar, packed	**½ cup**	**125 mL**
Liquid honey	**2 tbsp.**	**30 mL**
Butter or hard margarine	**½ cup**	**125 mL**
Soy sauce	**2 tsp.**	**10 mL**
Prepared mustard	**2 tsp.**	**10 mL**

Combine all 5 ingredients in small saucepan. Heat and stir until melted and blended. Makes about ¾ cup (175 mL).

HONEY SAUCE

Brush over chicken pieces during last stage of cooking.

Liquid honey	**⅓ cup**	**75 mL**
Prepared mustard	**1 tbsp.**	**15 mL**
Curry powder	**½ tsp.**	**2 mL**

Mix all 3 ingredients in small bowl. Makes ⅔ cup (150 mL).

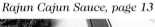

Rajun Cajun Sauce, page 13

RAJUN CAJUN SAUCE

More "rajun" (cayenne pepper) can be added to suite your taste.

Ketchup	⅔ cup	150 mL
Cayenne pepper	¼ tsp.	1 mL
Pepper	⅛ tsp.	0.5 mL
Garlic powder	⅛ tsp.	0.5 mL
Chili powder	⅛ tsp.	0.5 mL

Combine all 5 ingredients in small bowl. Makes ⅔ cup (150 mL).

Pictured on page 12.

BALI SAUCE

Resembles a sweet and sour sauce. Works well with chicken.

Brown sugar, packed	½ cup	125 mL
Granulated sugar	¼ cup	60 mL
Cornstarch	¼ cup	60 mL
Ground ginger	½ tsp.	2 mL
Salt	½ tsp.	2 mL
Pepper	¼ tsp.	1 mL
Water	1 cup	250 mL
White vinegar	½ cup	125 mL
Soy sauce	⅓ cup	75 mL

Stir first 6 ingredients together well in small saucepan.

Stir in water, vinegar and soy sauce. Heat and stir until sauce boils and thickens. Makes 2¼ cups (550 mL).

LEMON BASTING SAUCE

Use for marinating and basting chicken.

Lemon juice, fresh or bottled	1/3 cup	75 mL
Cooking oil	1/3 cup	75 mL
White wine vinegar	1/3 cup	75 mL
Soy sauce	1/2 tsp.	2 mL
Salt	1 tsp.	5 mL
Pepper	1/4 tsp.	1 mL
Ground thyme	1/4 tsp.	1 mL

Mix all 7 ingredients in saucepan. Heat and stir to boiling. Simmer 2 to 3 minutes. Makes about 1 cup (250 mL).

BASTING SAUCE

Brush on sirloin steak or cubes.

Ketchup	1/3 cup	75 mL
Cider vinegar	1/4 cup	60 mL
Soy sauce	2 tbsp.	30 mL
Mild molasses	2 tbsp.	30 mL

Combine all 4 ingredients in small bowl. Makes 3/4 cup (175 mL).

TIP

Keep a supply of natural bristle paint brushes for basting rather than more expensive basting brushes.

Also sometimes known as white sauces, cream sauces are most often served over pasta or seafood, but can also accompany beef, pork, poultry or vegetables. Start by creating a base sauce or roux (pronounced ROO) of flour and hot fat (butter, margarine or oil). Combine equal amounts of these two ingredients, or to keep your roux low-fat, use a ratio of ¾ part fat to 1 part flour. The result is a smooth, thick roux. Add milk or cream, any herbs or seasonings you wish, cheese, wine, sherry or chicken stock. The flavor of your sauce can be as distinctive as you want!

NUTTY SAUCE

Serve this over baked chicken or cooked broccoli florets.

Butter or hard margarine	2 tbsp.	30 mL
Sliced fresh mushrooms	2 cups	500 mL
All-purpose flour	2 tbsp.	30 mL
Salt	½ tsp.	2 mL
Pepper	¼ tsp.	1 mL
Garlic powder	¼ tsp.	1 mL
Apple juice	¾ cup	175 mL
Milk	1 cup	250 mL
Sliced hazelnuts, toasted in 350°F (175°C) oven about 5 minutes	3 tbsp.	50 mL

Melt butter in frying pan. Add mushrooms. Sauté until soft.

Mix in flour, salt, pepper and garlic powder. Stir in apple juice until mixture boils and thickens. Simmer until very thick.

Stir in milk and hazelnuts. Simmer about 2 minutes. Makes 2¾ cups (675 mL).

Pictured on page 19.

CREAM SAUCE

This basic white sauce recipe is so versatile. Try one or all of the variations.

Butter or hard margarine	2 tbsp.	30 mL
All-purpose flour	2 tbsp.	30 mL
Salt	¼ tsp.	1 mL
Pepper, sprinkle (or white pepper)		
Milk	1 cup	250 mL

Melt butter in saucepan. Mix in flour, salt and pepper. Add milk. Stir until sauce boils and thickens. Makes about 1 cup (250 mL).

CHEESE SAUCE: Add ½ cup (125 mL) grated medium or sharp Cheddar cheese to Cream Sauce. Amount may be varied. Or use about ¼ cup (60 mL) process cheese spread. More salt and cheese may be added if desired.

PARSLIED SAUCE: Add 2 tbsp. (30 mL) snipped fresh parsley to Cream Sauce or use 1½ tsp. (7 mL) parsley flakes.

PARMESAN SAUCE: Stir ⅓ cup (75 mL) grated Parmesan cheese into Cream Sauce.

CREAMED EGG SAUCE: Add 3 finely chopped hard-boiled eggs and 1 tsp. (5 mL) parsley flakes to Cream Sauce.

CREAM SAUCE

A slight variation of an old classic.

Butter or hard margarine	1½ tbsp.	25 mL
All-purpose flour	1½ tbsp.	25 mL
Salt	½ tsp.	2 mL
Pepper (or white pepper)	⅛ tsp.	0.5 mL
Large egg, fork-beaten	1	1
Milk	¾ cup	175 mL

Melt butter in medium saucepan. Mix in flour, salt and pepper. Remove from heat. Whisk in egg. Return to heat.

Stir in milk until sauce boils and thickens. Makes 1 cup (250 mL).

MUSHROOM SAUCE

Spoon over baked or fried chicken pieces.

Butter or hard margarine	2 tbsp.	30 mL
Sliced fresh mushrooms	2 cups	500 mL
All-purpose flour	2 tsp.	10 mL
Chicken bouillon powder	1 tsp.	5 mL
Paprika	1/8 tsp.	0.5 mL
Light cream	3/4 cup	175 mL
Soy sauce	1 tsp.	5 mL

Melt butter in frying pan. Add mushrooms. Sauté until soft.

Mix in flour, bouillon powder and paprika. Stir in cream and soy sauce until sauce boils and thickens slightly. Makes 2 cups (500 mL).

LEMON SAUCE

Serve over fish, seafood or poultry.

Butter or hard margarine	2 tbsp.	30 mL
All-purpose flour	2 tbsp.	30 mL
Salt	1/2 tsp.	2 mL
Pepper (white is best), sprinkle		
Onion powder	1/8 tsp.	0.5 mL
Milk	1 cup	250 mL
Lemon juice, fresh or bottled	2 tbsp.	30 mL
Butter or hard margarine, optional	2 tbsp.	30 mL
Large egg, optional	1	1

Melt first amount of butter in small saucepan. Mix in flour, salt, pepper and onion powder.

Add milk and lemon juice. Heat and stir until mixture boils and thickens. May be served now or add remaining ingredients.

Put sauce into blender. Add second amount of butter and egg. Blend until smooth. Return to saucepan. Heat and whisk until mixture starts to boil. If sauce curdles run through blender. Makes 1 cup (250 mL).

TIP

The secret to a smooth cream sauce is to mix the flour into the melted butter very well to produce a smooth roux. The milk or other liquid is then stirred in slowly over very low heat and allowed to thicken as you pour and stir.

DILL SAUCE

Basic cream sauce with the added dill. Serve over salmon loaf or salmon steaks.

Hard margarine (butter browns too fast)	**3 tbsp.**	**50 mL**
Finely chopped onion	**3 tbsp.**	**50 mL**
All-purpose flour	**3 tbsp.**	**50 mL**
Salt	**1/2 tsp.**	**2 mL**
Pepper	**1/8 tsp.**	**0.5 mL**
Milk	**1 1/2 cups**	**375 mL**
Dill weed	**1/4 tsp.**	**1 mL**

Melt margarine in saucepan. Add onion. Sauté until soft.

Mix in flour, salt and pepper. Stir in milk until sauce boils and thickens.

Add dill weed. Add more milk to thin sauce if desired. Makes 1 3/4 cups (425 mL).

DILL SAUCE

Tangier version. Serve over or with pork or on peas.

Butter or hard margarine	**2 tbsp.**	**30 mL**
All-purpose flour	**2 tbsp.**	**30 mL**
Dill weed	**1/2 tsp.**	**2 mL**
Chicken bouillon cubes	**2 × 1/5 oz.**	**2 × 6 g**
Boiling water	**1 1/2 cups**	**375 mL**
Sour cream	**1 cup**	**250 mL**

Melt butter in frying pan. Stir in flour and dill weed.

Dissolve bouillon cubes in water. Add and stir until sauce boils and thickens.

Add sour cream. Stir and heat through. Makes 2 1/2 cups (625 mL).

Pictured on page 19.

Top: Dill Sauce, page 18. Bottom: Nutty Sauce, page 15.

MUSTARD SAUCE

A must to serve with a ham loaf or patties or try with corned beef.

Chopped onion	$\frac{1}{3}$ cup	75 mL
Butter or hard margarine	2 tbsp.	30 mL
All-purpose flour	1 tbsp.	15 mL
Salt	$\frac{1}{4}$ tsp.	1 mL
Milk	1 cup	250 mL
Prepared mustard	1 tbsp.	15 mL
Lemon juice, fresh or bottled	1 tbsp.	15 mL

Sauté onion in butter in saucepan until soft.

Mix in flour and salt.

Add milk, mustard and lemon juice. Stir until sauce boils and thickens. Makes 1 cup (250 mL).

CURRY SAUCE

Use this instead of salt on broiled meat or fish. Low-sodium version.

Hard margarine (butter browns too fast)	1 tbsp.	15 mL
Finely chopped onion	$\frac{1}{3}$ cup	75 mL
All-purpose flour	4 tsp.	20 mL
Curry powder	1 tsp.	5 mL
Pepper	$\frac{1}{8}$ tsp.	0.5 mL
Envelope chicken bouillon powder (35% less salt)	1 × $\frac{1}{4}$ oz.	1 × 6.5 g
Water	$1\frac{1}{4}$ cups	300 mL

Melt margarine in frying pan. Add onion. Sauté until soft.

Sprinkle flour, curry powder, pepper and bouillon powder over onion. Mix. Stir in water. Heat and stir until sauce boils and thickens. Strain. Makes $\frac{3}{4}$ cup (175 mL).

PARÉ
pointer

He who laughs last

probably didn't get

the joke.

CARDAMOM SAUCE

The final touch-up for fried chicken or schnitzel.

Butter or hard margarine	1 tbsp.	15 mL
Finely chopped onion	3 tbsp.	50 mL
All-purpose flour	1 tbsp.	15 mL
Ground cardamom	$\frac{1}{4}$ tsp.	1 mL
Ground ginger	$\frac{1}{8}$ tsp.	0.5 mL
Pineapple juice	$\frac{1}{2}$ cup	125 mL
Soy sauce	1 tbsp.	15 mL

Melt butter in saucepan. Add onion. Sauté until soft.

Mix in flour, cardamom and ginger.

Stir in pineapple juice and soy sauce until sauce boils and thickens. Makes a scant $\frac{1}{2}$ cup (125 mL).

MUSHROOM SAUCE

Goes nicely with chicken, meatballs or meatloaf. This version uses water instead of milk or cream.

Butter or hard margarine	$\frac{1}{4}$ cup	60 mL
All-purpose flour	$\frac{1}{4}$ cup	60 mL
Salt	$\frac{1}{2}$ tsp.	2 mL
Pepper	$\frac{1}{8}$ tsp.	0.5 mL
Parsley flakes	1 tsp.	5 mL
Chicken bouillon powder	4 tsp.	20 mL
Worcestershire sauce	$\frac{1}{2}$ tsp.	2 mL
Paprika	$\frac{1}{2}$ tsp.	2 mL
Water	2 cups	500 mL
Canned sliced mushrooms, drained	$\frac{1}{2}$ cup	125 mL

Melt butter in saucepan over medium heat. Mix in flour, salt, pepper, parsley, bouillon powder, Worcestershire sauce and paprika. Stir in water and mushrooms until sauce boils and thickens. Makes 2 cups (500 mL).

SUNSHINE SAUCE

The cheery color comes from carrots. A winning combination. Serve over vegetables or pasta.

Butter or hard margarine	2 tbsp.	30 mL
Finely chopped onion	¼ cup	60 mL
Finely grated carrot	½ cup	125 mL
All-purpose flour	2 tbsp.	30 mL
Chicken bouillon powder	1 tsp.	5 mL
Water	1 cup	250 mL
Salt	¼ tsp.	1 mL

Melt butter in small saucepan. Add onion and carrot. Sauté until onion is soft and carrots are tender.

Mix in flour and bouillon powder. Stir in water and salt until sauce boils and thickens. Makes about 1 cup (250 mL).

MORNAY SAUCE

A mild sauce just right for fish fillets.

Butter or hard margarine	¼ cup	60 mL
All-purpose flour	¼ cup	60 mL
Chicken bouillon powder	1 tsp.	5 mL
Skim evaporated milk (or light cream)	13½ oz.	385 mL
Grated Parmesan cheese	⅓ cup	75 mL

Melt butter in saucepan. Mix in flour and bouillon powder. Stir in evaporated milk until mixture boils and thickens.

Add Parmesan cheese. Stir. Cover and remove from heat. Makes 2 cups (500 mL).

TIP

The color of the roux (and therefore the sauce) is determined by how long the flour is cooked in the butter. Flour will begin to darken after about 3 minutes and will be quite dark by about 10 minutes.

CRAB SAUCE

Serve over pasta, toast or in puffed pastry shells.

Butter or hard margarine	2 tbsp.	30 mL
All-purpose flour	2 tbsp.	30 mL
Salt	½ tsp.	2 mL
Pepper	¼ tsp.	1 mL
Garlic powder	⅛ tsp.	0.5 mL
Milk	1¼ cups	300 mL
Canned sliced mushrooms, drained	10 oz.	284 mL
Crabmeat (or 1 can, 4.2 oz., 120 g, drained), membrane removed	1 cup	250 mL
Grated medium Cheddar cheese	½ cup	125 mL
White wine (or alcohol-free wine), optional, but good	1 tbsp.	15 mL

Melt butter in saucepan. Mix in flour, salt, pepper and garlic powder. Stir in milk until mixture boils and thickens.

Stir in mushrooms, crabmeat, cheese and wine. Heat through. Cheese should be melted. Makes 2 cups (500 mL).

Pictured below.

SHRIMP SAUCE

Try over chicken or on pasta.

Butter or hard margarine	3 tbsp.	50 mL
All-purpose flour	3 tbsp.	50 mL
Salt	1/2 tsp.	2 mL
Pepper	1/8 tsp.	0.5 mL
Onion powder	1/8 tsp.	0.5 mL
Dill weed	1/8 tsp.	0.5 mL
Milk	1 cup	250 mL
Salad dressing (or mayonnaise)	1/4 cup	60 mL
Canned small shrimp, rinsed and drained	4 oz.	113 g

Melt butter in saucepan. Mix in flour, salt, pepper, onion powder and dill weed.

Stir in milk and salad dressing until sauce boils and thickens.

Carefully stir in shrimp. Heat through. Makes 1³/₄ cups (425 mL).

SHRIMP SAUCE

This special version turns any ordinary fish into something extraordinary.

Butter or hard margarine	2 tbsp.	30 mL
All-purpose flour	2 tbsp.	30 mL
Salt	1/4 tsp.	1 mL
Pepper	1/8 tsp.	0.5 mL
Chicken bouillon powder	1 tsp.	1 mL
Paprika	1/8 tsp.	0.5 mL
Milk	1 cup	250 mL
Small cooked shrimp (or 1 can, 4 oz., 113 g, rinsed and drained)	1 cup	250 mL
Sherry (or alcohol-free sherry)	2 tbsp.	30 mL

Melt butter in saucepan. Mix in flour, salt, pepper, bouillon powder and paprika. Stir in milk until mixture boils and thickens.

Add shrimp and sherry. Stir. Heat through. Makes 1¹/₂ cups (375 mL).

PARÉ *pointer*

Don't save money for a rainy day. It is a lot more fun to spend it in the sunshine.

LEMON SAUCE

Serve this microwave version with fish or vegetables.

Butter or hard margarine	**¼ cup**	**60 mL**
Finely chopped onion	**¼ cup**	**60 mL**
All-purpose flour	**3 tbsp.**	**50 mL**
Lemon juice, fresh or bottled	**2 tbsp.**	**30 mL**
Water	**¾ cup**	**175 mL**
Salt	**¼ tsp.**	**1 mL**
Pepper	**¹⁄₁₆ tsp.**	**0.5 mL**

Combine butter and onion in 4 cup (1 L) measuring cup. Microwave, uncovered, on high (100%) about 4 minutes or until tender. Stir at half time.

Mix in flour. Add remaining ingredients. Microwave, uncovered, on high (100%) about 2 minutes until mixture boils and thickens, stirring at 1 minute intervals. Makes generous 1 cup (250 mL).

Pictured below.

Was there ever a rolled crêpe, a bowl of fruit, a piece of cake or a scoop of ice cream that wasn't transformed from ordinary to exquisite by the addition of a velvety smooth, rich-tasting sauce? These sweet sauces range from custards to coulis (pronounced KOO-lee), from apricot to chocolate and from creamy smooth to hard. Make your favorite sauce ahead of time and freeze (with the exception of egg-based custards).

DELUXE CHOCOLATE SAUCE

This delicious sauce keeps for ages. A real treat to have on hand. Serve over ice cream.

Semisweet chocolate chips	2 cups	500 mL
Butter or hard margarine	½ cup	125 mL
Instant coffee granules	1 tbsp.	15 mL
Salt	⅛ tsp.	0.5 mL
Vanilla	1 tbsp.	15 mL
Icing (confectioner's) sugar	2 cups	500 mL
Light corn syrup	1 cup	250 mL
Hot water	1 cup	250 mL

Measure first 5 ingredients into saucepan. Heat and stir on medium until smooth. Remove from heat.

Beat in icing sugar, syrup and water until smooth. Pour into jar. Store in refrigerator. Makes 4½ cups (1.1 L).

Pictured on page 27.

Clockwise from top right: Blueberry Sauce, page 38; Maple Walnut Sauce, page 30; and Deluxe Chocolate Sauce, page 26.

HOT FUDGE SAUCE

Very chocolaty, dark and smooth. Pour over ice cream or pound cake.

Granulated sugar	1 cup	250 mL
Cocoa	½ cup	125 mL
Salt, pinch		
Evaporated milk	⅔ cup	150 mL
Butter or hard margarine	¼ cup	60 mL
Vanilla	1 tsp.	5 mL

Measure all 6 ingredients into heavy saucepan. Heat and stir until mixture comes to a rolling boil that can't be stirred down. Start timing. Continue to stir for 1 minute. Sauce will be thick. Makes 1½ cups (375 mL).

Pictured on this page.

CHOCOLATE SAUCE

Serve hot or cold. If serving cold, stir in a bit more milk to desired consistency. So quick in the microwave.

Semisweet chocolate chips	1 cup	250 mL
Milk	⅓ cup	75 mL
Vanilla	¼ tsp.	1 mL
Grand Marnier liqueur, optional, but good	2 tsp.	10 mL

Combine all 4 ingredients in 2 cup (500 mL) measuring cup. Microwave, uncovered, on high (100%) for about 2 minutes until melted and smooth, stirring after 1 minute. Makes ⅞ cup (220 mL).

CHOCOLATE FONDUE SAUCE

Only three ingredients in this smooth-as-satin topping. Serve hot or cold.

Evaporated milk	1 cup	250 mL
Semisweet chocolate chips	1½ cups	375 mL
Vanilla	1 tsp.	5 mL

Put milk, chips and vanilla into saucepan. Melt over medium heat until chips combine when stirred. Remove from heat. Makes 1⅔ cups (400 mL).

CHOCOLATE WHIPPED CREAM

Great as a topping on a slice of angel food cake.

Whipping cream (or 1 env. topping)	1 cup	250 mL
Granulated sugar	2 tsp.	10 mL
Cocoa	2 tbsp.	30 mL
Vanilla	½ tsp.	2 mL

Beat cream in small bowl until fairly thick. Add sugar, cocoa and vanilla. Beat until stiff. Makes 2 cups (500 mL).

CHOCO PEANUT BUTTER TOPPING

Always serve this sauce hot. It gets very thick when cold.

Semisweet chocolate chips	1 cup	250 mL
Smooth peanut butter	½ cup	125 mL
Evaporated milk	⅓ cup	75 mL
Corn syrup	¼ cup	60 mL

Combine all 4 ingredients in saucepan. Heat and stir until chips are melted. Makes 1 cup (250 mL).

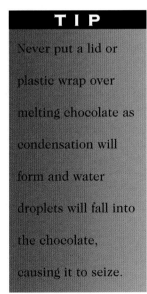

TIP

Never put a lid or plastic wrap over melting chocolate as condensation will form and water droplets will fall into the chocolate, causing it to seize.

MAPLE WALNUT SAUCE

Thick and nutty. A natural to spoon over ice cream. Ready in under 10 minutes in the microwave.

Brown sugar, packed	1 cup	250 mL
All-purpose flour	¼ cup	60 mL
Water	1½ cups	375 mL
Corn syrup	2 tbsp.	30 mL
Butter or hard margarine	2 tbsp.	30 mL
Maple flavoring	1 tsp.	5 mL
Chopped walnuts	1 cup	250 mL

Combine sugar and flour in 4 cup (1 L) measuring cup. Stir well.

Mix in water. Add remaining ingredients. Stir. Microwave, uncovered, on high (100%) for about 2 minutes. Stir. Cook and stir every minute for about 4 minutes more until sauce boils and thickens. Makes 2⅔ cups (650 mL).

Pictured on page 27.

MAPLE NUT SAUCE

Quick to make. Store in refrigerator up to three weeks. Serve over ice cream.

Sweetened condensed milk	11 oz.	300 mL
Chopped pecans or walnuts	2 tbsp.	30 mL
Maple flavoring	½ tsp.	2 mL

Stir milk, pecans and maple flavoring together in bowl. Makes 1½ cups (375 mL).

PARÉ
pointer

A seafood diet is the

best. Whenever you

see food, eat it.

BUTTERSCOTCH SAUCE

So good over ice cream.

Brown sugar, packed	**1½ cups**	**375 mL**
All-purpose flour	**1 tbsp.**	**15 mL**
Dark corn syrup	**½ cup**	**125 mL**
Butter or hard margarine	**2 tbsp.**	**30 mL**
Salt	**⅛ tsp.**	**0.5 mL**
Evaporated milk	**1 cup**	**250 mL**

Put sugar and flour into saucepan. Stir well.

Add rest of ingredients. Heat and stir on medium until sauce starts to boil. Remove from heat. Sauce thickens when it cools. Store, covered, in refrigerator. Makes $1\frac{7}{8}$ cups (470 mL).

Pictured on this page.

PEANUT BUTTER SAUCE

A treat for ice cream.

Granulated sugar	**1 cup**	**250 mL**
All-purpose flour	**¼ cup**	**60 mL**
Milk	**¾ cup**	**175 mL**
Smooth peanut butter	**⅓ cup**	**75 mL**
Corn syrup	**1 tbsp.**	**15 mL**

Measure sugar and flour into saucepan. Stir well.

Add next 3 ingredients. Mix thoroughly. Place over medium heat stirring until sauce boils. Remove from heat. Cool. Makes 1½ cups (375 mL).

CUSTARD SAUCE

Spoon over coffee cake.

Custard powder	**1 tbsp.**	**15 mL**
Granulated sugar	**1 tbsp.**	**15 mL**
Milk	**1 cup**	**250 mL**
Vanilla	**½ tsp.**	**2 mL**

Stir custard powder and sugar together well in saucepan. Mix in milk and vanilla. Heat and stir until sauce boils and thickens. Makes 1 cup (250 mL).

Pictured on page 33.

BROWN SUGAR SAUCE

The finishing touch for warm freshly baked white cake and all steamed fruit puddings.

Brown sugar, packed	**1 cup**	**250 mL**
All-purpose flour	**¼ cup**	**60 mL**
Salt	**½ tsp.**	**2 mL**
Water	**2 cups**	**500 mL**
Vanilla	**1 tsp.**	**5 mL**

Mix brown sugar, flour and salt in medium saucepan. This enables water to be mixed in with no lumps.

Stir in water and vanilla. Heat and stir over medium until sauce boils and thickens. Makes about 2½ cups (625 mL).

RUM SAUCE: Add 1 tsp. (5 mL) rum flavoring. Dark brown sugar is best for this.

RUM RAISIN SAUCE: Add 1 tsp. (5 mL) rum flavoring, ½ cup (125 mL) raisins and 2 tsp. (10 mL) grated lemon peel. Adding ½ cup (125 mL) chopped pecans is extra special.

CHOCOLATE PUDDING SAUCE: Mix in 1½ tbsp. (25 mL) cocoa with sugar mixture.

VANILLA PUDDING SAUCE: Use granulated sugar instead of brown sugar.

CHRISTMAS PUDDING SAUCE

Beautiful caramel color with perfect blend of flavors. Serve with your favorite Christmas pudding.

Brown sugar, packed	½ **cup**	**125 mL**
Granulated sugar	½ **cup**	**125 mL**
Cornstarch	**3 tbsp.**	**50 mL**
Water	**1 cup**	**250 mL**
Butter or hard margarine	¼ **cup**	**60 mL**
Lemon juice, fresh or bottled	**2 tbsp.**	**30 mL**
Rum flavoring	**1 tsp.**	**5 mL**

Mix both sugars and cornstarch in saucepan.

Add water. Stir. Add butter, lemon juice and rum flavoring. Heat and stir until sauce boils and thickens. Makes 1⅔ cups (400 mL).

Custard Sauce, page 32

BRANDY HARD SAUCE

Have this instead of a pourable sauce. Serve with fruited steamed pudding.

Butter or hard margarine	½ cup	125 mL
Brown sugar, packed	1 cup	250 mL
Vanilla	1 tsp.	5 mL
Brandy flavoring	½ tsp.	2 mL

Microwave butter in a small bowl on high (100%) for about 20 seconds to soften. Add next 3 ingredients. Beat well. Cover and chill until needed. Makes 1 cup (250 mL).

Pictured on page 35.

PASTEL HARD SAUCE

Try a variety of colors and shapes. Make well in advance and store in fridge. Layer between waxed paper.

Butter or hard margarine, softened	¼ cup	60 mL
Icing (confectioner's) sugar	1 cup	250 mL
Vanilla or brandy flavoring	1 tsp.	5 mL
Milk, for thinning		
Food coloring, if desired		

Beat butter, icing sugar and vanilla together. Add a bit of milk if needed, to make a touch softer. Work in food coloring with hands. Spread about ¼ inch (6 mm) thick on cookie sheet. Roll to smooth. Chill. Use cookie cutter to cut into Christmas trees, stars or balls. Remove with lifter. Soften scraps to room temperature. Repeat. Makes a scant 1 cup (250 mL).

PARÉ
pointer

Of course you know

that a musician

cleans his tuba with

tuba toothpaste.

Brandy Hard Sauce, page 34

RASPBERRY COULIS

Try koo-LEE for a picture perfect dessert. Pour onto plate before or after dessert is placed on plate.

Frozen raspberries, in syrup, thawed	**15 oz.**	**425 g**
Reserved syrup		
Granulated sugar	**2 tbsp.**	**30 mL**
Cornstarch	**4 tsp.**	**20 mL**

Strain raspberries through sieve. Reserve syrup. Discard pulp and seeds.

Measure syrup. There will be about 1 cup (250 mL). Add water to make 1¼ cups (300 mL). Pour into saucepan.

Mix in sugar and cornstarch. Heat and stir until sauce boils and thickens. Cool. Makes 1¼ cups (300 mL).

Pictured on page 37.

STRAWBERRY COULIS: Use frozen sliced strawberries in syrup rather than raspberries.

Clockwise from top left: Raspberry Coulis, page 35;
Orange Sauce, page 36; and Apricot Sauce, page 39.

ORANGE SAUCE

Soft and fluffy. Pile on a slice of angel food or chocolate cake or spoon over a crêpe, a wedge of cheesecake or into a chocolate cup.

Egg yolk (large)	1	1
Frozen concentrated orange juice, thawed	½ cup	125 mL
Water	1 cup	250 mL
Grated orange peel	1 tsp.	5 mL
Lemon juice, fresh or bottled	2 tsp.	10 mL
Butter or hard margarine	1 tbsp.	15 mL
Granulated sugar	⅔ cup	150 mL
All-purpose flour	2 tbsp.	30 mL
Salt	¼ tsp.	1 mL
Water	¼ cup	60 mL
Egg white (large), room temperature	1	1
Whipping cream	1 cup	250 mL

Beat egg yolk with a spoon in heavy saucepan. Add concentrated orange juice gradually. Stir in first amount of water, peel, lemon juice and butter. Heat over medium until boiling.

Stir sugar, flour and salt together. Mix in second amount of water. Pour into orange mixture, stirring until mixture boils and thickens. Cool.

Beat egg white until stiff. Using same beaters, beat cream until stiff. Fold egg white into cooled mixture then fold in whipped cream. Makes 3½ cups (875 mL).

Pictured on page 37.

SIMPLE ORANGE SAUCE

A good make-ahead that stores well.

Prepared orange juice	1 cup	250 mL
Cornstarch	2 tbsp.	30 mL
Granulated sugar	¾ cup	175 mL
Grated orange peel	1 tsp.	5 mL

Mix all 4 ingredients in saucepan. Heat and stir over medium until sauce boils and thickens. Makes 1¼ cups (300 mL).

BLUEBERRY SAUCE

Good over crêpes, waffles or ice cream.

Blueberries, fresh or frozen	10 oz.	284 g
Water	½ cup	125 mL
Granulated sugar	½ cup	125 mL
Cornstarch	1 tbsp.	15 mL
Lemon juice, fresh or bottled	1 tbsp.	15 mL

Combine all 5 ingredients together in saucepan. Stir well. Heat and stir over medium until boiling. Simmer gently for about 5 minutes until berries release their juice. Makes 2 cups (500 mL).

Pictured on page 27.

LEMON SAUCE

The perfect complement to cheesecake or for serving over warm gingerbread.

Granulated sugar	½ cup	125 mL
Water	1 cup	250 mL
Lemon juice, fresh or bottled	3 tbsp.	50 mL
Grated lemon peel	1 tsp.	5 mL
Butter or hard margarine	1 tbsp.	15 mL
Salt	⅛ tsp.	0.5 mL
Water	¼ cup	60 mL
Cornstarch	4 tsp.	20 mL

Combine first 6 ingredients in saucepan. Heat and stir to boiling.

Mix water with cornstarch. Stir into hot mixture. Cook and stir until thickened. Cool. Makes 1½ cups (375 mL).

PARÉ *pointer*

Even if your dreams

don't come true, be

thankful that your

nightmares don't

either.

PINEAPPLE SAUCE

For a thicker, more fruity sauce, simply omit extra pineapple juice.

Canned crushed pineapple, with juice	**14 oz.**	**398 mL**
Pineapple juice	**1 cup**	**250 mL**
Granulated sugar	**⅓ cup**	**75 mL**
Cornstarch	**4 tsp.**	**20 mL**

Mix all 4 ingredients in saucepan. Heat and stir until sauce boils and thickens. Makes 2¾ cups (675 mL).

Pictured on this page.

PINEAPPLE SAUCE

You will love this tangier version. Chill and use as a fruit dip.

Pineapple juice	**¼ cup**	**60 mL**
Cornstarch	**2 tbsp.**	**30 mL**
White vinegar	**¼ cup**	**60 mL**
Granulated sugar	**¼ cup**	**60 mL**

Put pineapple juice, cornstarch, vinegar and sugar into small saucepan. Bring to a boil over medium heat, stirring continuously, to thicken. Makes about ½ cup (125 mL).

APRICOT SAUCE

Serve hot or cold over crêpes, ice cream or cake.

Apricot jam	**1 cup**	**250 mL**
Prepared orange juice	**2 tbsp.**	**30 mL**
Brandy flavoring	**½ tsp.**	**2 mL**

Mix all 3 ingredients in small bowl. Makes 1 cup (250 mL).

Pictured on page 37.

FRUIT SAUCE

So quick and simple. Surround with bite-size pieces of fruit.

Cream cheese, softened	8 oz.	250 g
Granulated sugar, corn syrup or honey	¼ cup	60 mL
Prepared orange juice	½ cup	125 mL

Beat all 3 ingredients together. Add more orange juice if needed to thin sauce a bit more, although there will be some juice on the fruit so don't make it too thin. Makes a scant 2 cups (500 mL).

FRUIT TOPPING

Just right to top off any fruit dessert or use as a fruit dip. So easy.

Whipping cream (or 1 env. topping)	1 cup	250 mL
Raspberry-flavored yogurt	1 cup	250 mL

Beat cream until stiff. Mix in yogurt. Makes 3 cups (750 mL).

EASY FRUIT SAUCE

Use as a topping or dip.

Plain yogurt or sour cream	1 cup	250 mL
Brown sugar, packed	2 tbsp.	30 mL
Grated orange peel (or 1 tbsp., 15 mL, Kahlua liqueur)	1 tsp.	5 mL

Stir all 3 ingredients together well. Makes a generous 1 cup (250 mL).

TIP

Toppings that use whipped cream should be served within 3 to 4 hours before the cream begins to separate and "weep". Prepared powdered toppings can be substituted in many cases and will allow a longer standing time.

Fruit sauces are natural partners to the distinctive flavors of beef, pork, fish and poultry. Many of these simple recipes contain vinegar or lemon juice to balance the natural sweetness of the fruit, resulting in a sauce that is both sweet and tangy. You will be pleased with the delightful flavors these sauces can bring to your food.

PLUM SAUCE

Sauce will be dark or light depending on whether you use regular plum or greengage jam. Very tasty over egg rolls or chicken.

Plum jam	1 cup	250 mL
Cider vinegar	3 tbsp.	50 mL
Granulated sugar	2 tsp.	10 mL

Stir all 3 ingredients together. If mixture contains a lot of skins, put through a sieve. Makes generous 1 cup (250 mL).

Pictured below.

Left: Orange Sauce, page 42. Right: Plum Sauce, page 41.

ORANGE ONION SAUCE

Serve with baked salmon steaks or fillets.

Water	¼ cup	60 mL
Prepared orange juice	2 tbsp.	30 mL
Red wine vinegar	2 tbsp.	30 mL
Chopped green onion	3 tbsp.	50 mL
Beef bouillon powder	½ tsp.	2 mL

Stir all 5 ingredients together in small saucepan. Bring to a boil, stirring often. Boil until about ½ is evaporated. Makes about ¼ cup (60 mL).

ORANGE SAUCE

Spoon warm sauce over Cornish hens or baked chicken pieces.

Prepared orange juice	1 cup	250 mL
Granulated sugar	¼ cup	60 mL
Lemon juice, fresh or bottled	1 tbsp.	15 mL
Grated orange peel	1 tsp.	5 mL
Cornstarch	1 tbsp.	15 mL
Water	1 tbsp.	15 mL

Combine first 4 ingredients in small saucepan over medium heat. Bring to a boil.

Mix cornstarch and water. Stir into sauce until it boils and thickens. Makes 1¼ cups (300 mL).

Pictured on page 41.

PARÉ
pointer

Their telephone bill

proves that talk isn't

cheap.

APPLESAUCE

Homemade is definitely the best. Use hot or cold.

Medium cooking apples (Mcintosh is good), peeled, cored and sliced	4	4
Water	½ **cup**	125 mL
Granulated sugar	¼ **cup**	60 mL
Ground cinnamon (optional)		

Put apple and water into saucepan. Bring to a boil. Cover and simmer gently until apple is soft. Stir occasionally.

Mix in sugar. Remove from heat. Taste. Add more sugar if needed and add a bit more water if you want a thinner sauce. For a cinnamon flavor, stir in a small amount to taste while sauce is hot. Makes about 2 cups (500 mL).

CRANBERRY APPLESAUCE

Goes with chicken, goose, duck or any other feathered relatives. Also good with pork.

Medium cooking apples (McIntosh is good), peeled, cored and sliced	5	5
Cranberries, fresh or frozen	2 cups	500 mL
Brown sugar, packed	1 cup	250 mL
Ground cinnamon	¼ tsp.	1 mL
Ground ginger	⅛ tsp.	0.5 mL

Put all 5 ingredients into saucepan. Heat, stirring often, until sauce comes to a boil. Simmer for 25 minutes. Makes about 2½ cups (625 mL).

GINGER PEACH SAUCE

Serve over any poached, baked or fried fish fillets. Good spooned over fish steaks as well.

Canned sliced peaches, with juice	**14 oz.**	**398 mL**
Frozen concentrated orange juice	**1 tbsp.**	**15 mL**
Lemon juice, fresh or bottled	**1 tbsp.**	**15 mL**
Ground ginger	**½ tsp.**	**2 mL**
Cornstarch	**1 tbsp.**	**15 mL**

Place all 5 ingredients in blender. Process until smooth. Pour into saucepan. Heat and stir until sauce boils and thickens. Makes 1⅔ cups (400 mL).

RAISIN SAUCE

Serve with baked ham or a pork roast.

Raisins	**½ cup**	**125 mL**
Hot water	**2 cups**	**500 mL**
Brown sugar, packed	**1⅓ cups**	**325 mL**
Cornstarch	**¼ cup**	**60 mL**
Water	**½ cup**	**125 mL**
White vinegar	**3 tbsp.**	**50 mL**
Dry mustard powder	**¼ tsp.**	**1 mL**

Put raisins and hot water into medium saucepan. Let stand 1 hour.

Stir in brown sugar and cornstarch. Add water, vinegar and mustard. Heat and stir over medium until sauce boils and thickens. Makes 2 cups (500 mL).

PARÉ
pointer

A newly hatched

beetle is called a

baby buggy.

Here is a popular appetizer or main course dish made unique by your choice of sauce. Meatballs are convenient because they can either be browned in advance and later served with your sauce or cooked directly in the sauce you have prepared. Double the recipe and have enough left over to serve over rice, potatoes or pasta!

MUSTARD SAUCE

Delicious served with meatballs or over ham.

All-purpose flour	2 tbsp.	30 mL
Skim milk	¾ cup	175 mL
Skim milk powder	⅓ cup	75 mL
Prepared mustard	3½ tsp.	17 mL
Onion powder	¼ tsp.	1 mL
White vinegar	4 tsp.	20 mL
Liquid sweetener (or 1 tbsp., 15 mL granulated sugar)	1 tsp.	5 mL
Salt	⅛ tsp.	0.5 mL

Mix flour with part of milk until smooth. Add rest of milk along with remaining ingredients. Heat and stir until sauce boils and thickens. Chill until needed. Reheat to serve. Makes ¾ cup (175 mL).

APPETIZER MEATBALL SAUCES

Pour these sauces over tiny meatballs in a chafing dish or other warming dish. Serve with cocktail picks.

PEANUT SAUCE

Smooth peanut butter	¼ cup	60 mL
Water	½ cup	125 mL
Brown sugar, packed	2 tbsp.	30 mL
Soy sauce	1 tbsp.	15 mL
Lemon juice, fresh or bottled	2 tsp.	10 mL
Crushed red chilies	½ tsp.	2 mL
Garlic powder (or 1 clove, minced)	¼ tsp.	1 mL

Mix all 7 ingredients in saucepan. Simmer for 5 minutes. Makes ¾ cup (175 mL).

MUSHROOM BARBECUE SAUCE

Condensed cream of mushroom soup	10 oz.	284 mL
Soup can full of barbecue sauce	10 oz.	284 mL

Combine soup and sauce in small saucepan. Heat and stir. Makes 2¼ cups (550 mL).

MUSHROOM CHEESE SAUCE

Condensed cream of mushroom soup	10 oz.	284 mL
Cream cheese	8 oz.	250 g
Milk	½ cup	125 mL

Heat and stir all 3 ingredients together in saucepan. Makes 2½ cups (625 mL).

RED SWEET SAUCE

Chili sauce	1 cup	250 mL
Mild molasses	¼ cup	60 mL
White vinegar	¼ cup	60 mL

Heat and stir all 3 ingredients in saucepan. Makes 1½ cups (375 mL).

CHILI GRAPE SAUCE

Chili sauce	1¼ cups	300 mL
Grape jelly	1 cup	250 mL
Lemon juice, fresh or bottled	1 tsp.	5 mL

Mix all 3 ingredients in saucepan. Simmer for 5 minutes. Makes 2¼ cups (560 mL).

TOMATO SAUCE

Tomato sauce	7½ oz.	213 mL
Ketchup	½ cup	125 mL
Sweet pickle relish	2 tbsp.	30 mL
Brown sugar, packed	2 tbsp.	30 mL
White vinegar	1 tbsp.	15 mL
Dry onion flakes	2 tsp.	10 mL
Worcestershire sauce	1 tsp.	5 mL

Heat and stir all 7 ingredients in saucepan. Makes 2 cups (500 mL).

TOMATO CHILI SAUCE

Canned tomatoes, with juice, broken up	2 × 14 oz.	2 × 398 mL
Chili powder	2 tsp.	10 mL
Salt	1 tsp.	5 mL

Heat and stir all 3 ingredients in saucepan. Makes ¾ cup (175 mL).

SWEET AND SOUR SAUCE

Use as an appetizer sauce for dunking meatballs.

Brown sugar, packed	1 cup	250 mL
Cornstarch	2 tbsp.	30 mL
White vinegar	½ cup	125 mL
Pineapple juice (or water)	½ cup	125 mL

Stir sugar and cornstarch together in saucepan. Add vinegar and pineapple juice. Bring to a boil over medium heat stirring constantly until mixture thickens. Makes 1⅓ cups (325 mL).

SWEET AND SOUR SAUCE

Dark and delicious over meatballs or ribs.

Brown sugar, packed	2 cups	500 mL
All-purpose flour	2 tsp.	10 mL
White vinegar	½ cup	125 mL
Water	⅓ cup	75 mL
Soy sauce	2 tbsp.	30 mL
Ketchup	2 tbsp.	30 mL

Thoroughly mix brown sugar and flour in small saucepan. Stir in vinegar, water, soy sauce and ketchup. Heat and stir over medium until sauce boils and thickens. Makes ¾ cup (175 mL).

SWEET AND SOUR LIGHT

Named for its color—nice and light.

Granulated sugar	1 cup	250 mL
Water	¾ cup	175 mL
White vinegar	¾ cup	175 mL
Cornstarch	2 tbsp.	30 mL
Paprika	1 tsp.	5 mL
Salt	½ tsp.	2 mL

Combine all 6 ingredients in saucepan. Heat and stir. Makes 1¾ cups (425 mL).

TIP

Freeze meatballs separately from the sauce so the sauce can be reheated and stirred before combining with meatballs.

These wonderful, savory sauces suit practically any dish you choose to make. All are easy to prepare and many don't require warming or cooking. Simply mix, stir and serve (but don't freeze).

SEAFOOD COCKTAIL SAUCE

Perfect for shrimp and other seafood.

Tomato paste	¼ cup	60 mL
Light salad dressing (or mayonnaise)	¼ cup	60 mL
Skim milk	¼ cup	60 mL
Lemon juice, fresh or bottled	1 tsp.	5 mL
Worcestershire sauce	½ tsp.	2 mL
Prepared horseradish	½ tsp.	2 mL

Mix all 6 ingredients in small bowl. A little more horseradish may be used if you wish. Store in refrigerator. Makes ¾ cup (175 mL).

SEAFOOD SAUCE

Sauce is just right for traditional shrimp cocktail appetizer.

Chili sauce	½ cup	125 mL
Ketchup	⅓ cup	75 mL
Sweet pickle relish	2 tbsp.	30 mL
Prepared horseradish	1 tsp.	5 mL
Worcestershire sauce	½ tsp.	2 mL
Lemon juice, fresh or bottled	½ tsp.	2 mL
Seasoned salt	¼ tsp.	1 mL

Stir all 7 ingredients together in small bowl. Chill until ready to assemble. Makes ¾ cup (175 mL).

Pictured on this page.

DILLED SAUCE

No cooking required. Serve with any fish or seafood. May be used immediately, but flavor is better after refrigerated for an hour.

Sour cream	1 cup	250 mL
Salad dressing (or mayonnaise)	1 cup	250 mL
Milk	¼ cup	60 mL
Prepared horseradish	1 tbsp.	15 mL
Dry mustard powder	½ tsp.	2 mL
Dill weed	½ tsp.	2 mL
Granulated sugar	¼ tsp.	1 mL
Salt	½ tsp.	2 mL

Mix all 8 ingredients well. Makes a generous 2 cups (500 mL).

CUCUMBER SAUCE

Good with any fish.

Sour cream	½ cup	125 mL
Salad dressing (or mayonnaise)	¼ cup	60 mL
Chives	2 tsp.	10 mL
Parsley flakes	2 tsp.	10 mL
Lemon juice, fresh or bottled	1 tsp.	5 mL
Salt	¼ tsp.	1 mL
Onion powder	¼ tsp.	1 mL
Medium cucumber, with peel, halved lengthwise, seeded and grated	1	1

Mix first 7 ingredients in small bowl. Chill.

Drain grated cucumber thoroughly. Add to sour cream mixture shortly before serving so it doesn't cause sauce to go watery. Makes about 1⅓ cups (325 mL).

Pictured on page 52.

· P A R É
pointer

Growing older is like

making pudding.

You get lumps if you

don't stir.

TARTAR SAUCE

No fish is complete without it.

Salad dressing (or mayonnaise)	**1 cup**	**250 mL**
Chopped dill pickle (or sweet pickle relish)	**¼ cup**	**60 mL**
Lemon juice, fresh or bottled	**1 tbsp.**	**15 mL**
Chopped pimiento (or chopped stuffed olives)	**1 tsp.**	**5 mL**
Parsley flakes	**1 tsp.**	**5 mL**
Onion powder	**⅛ tsp.**	**0.5 mL**

Mix all 6 ingredients in small bowl. Chill until needed. Makes 1¼ cups (300 mL).

TARTAR DILL SAUCE

Good for mushroom or fish dipping.

Salad dressing (or mayonnaise)	**¾ cup**	**175 mL**
Sweet pickle relish	**¼ cup**	**60 mL**
Lemon juice, fresh or bottled	**1 tbsp.**	**15 mL**
Dill weed	**½ tsp.**	**2 mL**

Mix all 4 ingredients in small bowl. Makes 1 cup (250 mL).

CURRY SAUCE

Smooth sauce that can be served hot with chicken. Try as a dressing with cold cooked rice or pasta.

Salad dressing (or mayonnaise)	**1 cup**	**250 mL**
Curry powder	**1 tbsp.**	**15 mL**
Lemon juice, fresh or bottled	**½ tsp.**	**2 mL**
Paprika	**½ tsp.**	**2 mL**
Onion powder	**⅛ tsp.**	**0.5 mL**

Mix all 5 ingredients in small bowl. Makes 1 cup (250 mL).

Pictured on page 52.

MOCK HOLLANDAISE

A foolproof microwave method. Drizzle over asparagus, broccoli or other vegetables.

Sour cream	¹⁄₂ cup	125 mL
Salad dressing (or mayonnaise)	¹⁄₂ cup	125 mL
Lemon juice, fresh or bottled	2 tsp.	10 mL
Prepared mustard	1 tsp.	5 mL

Combine all 4 ingredients in 2 cup (500 mL) glass measuring cup. Stir. Microwave, uncovered, on high (100%) about 2 minutes until hot, stirring after 1 minute. Makes 1 cup (250 mL).

HOLLANDAISE SAUCE

A smooth shrimp and mushroom sauce. Serve over baked fish fillets.

Egg yolks (large)	3	3
Butter or hard margarine, melted	1 cup	250 mL
Lemon juice, fresh or bottled	1 tbsp.	15 mL
Chopped cooked shrimp	1 cup	250 mL
Finely chopped fresh mushrooms	¹⁄₂ cup	125 mL
Paprika	¹⁄₄ tsp.	1 mL
Salt	¹⁄₄ tsp.	1 mL
Pepper	¹⁄₈ tsp.	0.5 mL

Put egg yolks into top of double boiler over hot, not boiling, water. Stir. Add melted butter very slowly, stirring continuously until thickened. Add lemon juice. Stir.

Add shrimp and mushrooms. Stir in paprika, salt and pepper. Heat through. Makes 2¹⁄₄ cups (560 mL).

TIP

To prevent Hollandaise from breaking down, it must be cooked over very low heat and stirred slowly.

Top: Cucumber Sauce, page 50. Bottom: Curry Sauce, page 51.

RED PEPPER SAUCE

Serve over pasta or fish fillets.

Hard margarine (butter browns too fast)	2 tbsp.	30 mL
Red pepper, finely chopped	1	1
Chopped green onion	¼ cup	60 mL
Skim evaporated milk (or whipping cream)	1 cup	250 mL
Salt	½ tsp.	2 mL
Cornstarch	1 tbsp.	15 mL
Water	2 tbsp.	30 mL

Melt margarine in small saucepan. Add red pepper and green onion. Sauté until soft.

Add evaporated milk. Stir. Bring to a boil.

Mix salt and cornstarch with water in small cup. Stir into sauce until it boils and thickens. Makes 1¾ cups (425 mL).

PARSLEY SAUCE

Just the right sharpness to serve with fish. This can be used instead of a tartar sauce.

Salad dressing (or mayonnaise)	1 cup	250 mL
Red wine vinegar	2 tbsp.	30 mL
Lemon juice, fresh or bottled	2 tbsp.	30 mL
Milk	2 tbsp.	30 mL
Parsley flakes	1 tbsp.	15 mL
Salt	½ tsp.	2 mL
Pepper	⅛ tsp.	0.5 mL

Mix all 7 ingredients well. Chill overnight so flavors blend. May be served cold as a dip, or warm as a sauce. Makes 1⅔ cups (400 mL).

PARÉ *pointer*

How come opportunity

rarely knocks but

temptation pounds

away every day?

HORSERADISH SAUCE

Instead of the usual plain horseradish, set this beside the beef.

Salad dressing (or mayonnaise)	1 cup	250 mL
Sour cream	½ cup	125 mL
Finely chopped green onion	2 tbsp.	30 mL
Prepared horseradish	1½ tbsp.	25 mL
Salt	½ tsp.	2 mL
Pepper	⅛ tsp.	0.5 mL

Measure all 6 ingredients into small bowl. Mix to blend. Makes 1½ cups (375 mL).

Variation: Mix in ¼ tsp. (1 mL) curry powder.

STROGANOFF SAUCE

Serve over broad noodles or meatballs.

Water	1¼ cups	300 mL
Cornstarch	4 tsp.	25 mL
Beef bouillon powder	1 tbsp.	15 mL
Sliced fresh mushrooms, sautéed	¼ cup	60 mL
Sour cream	⅔ cup	175 mL

Combine all 5 ingredients in saucepan. Heat and stir until boiling. Makes 2 cups (500 mL).

MINT SAUCE

Serve hot with lamb.

Dried mint leaves, crumbled	1 tbsp.	15 mL
Boiling water	¼ cup	60 mL
White vinegar	2 tbsp.	30 mL
Granulated sugar	2 tsp.	10 mL

Put all 4 ingredients into small saucepan. Bring to a boil. Simmer about 2 minutes. Makes ⅓ cup (75 mL).

These three quick cheese sauces are great served with fish, vegetables, steak or pasta. You should plan to make your sauce beforehand so that it can sit at least 4 hours in the refrigerator. Time will allow flavors to blend and become more distinctive. Expecting a lot of guests? Just double or triple the recipe and you have a successful meal!

CHEESE SAUCE

A quick, easy sauce. Mellow. Adds greatly to fish.

Condensed cream of mushroom soup	10 oz.	284 mL
Grated medium Cheddar cheese	½ cup	125 mL
Cream or milk	2 tbsp.	30 mL

Mix soup, cheese and cream together in small saucepan. Place on edge of barbecue grill or over low heat on stove. Makes 1⅓ cups (325 mL).

BLUE CHEESE SAUCE

Mellow with a fairly mild cheese flavor. Serve with any fish, or put a dollop on steak.

Sour cream	1 cup	250 mL
Cream cheese, softened	4 oz.	125 g
Blue cheese, crumbled	3 tbsp.	50 mL
Onion salt	¼ tsp.	1 mL

Combine all 4 ingredients in bowl. Beat until very well mixed. Chill. Makes about 1½ cups (375 mL).

PARMESAN SAUCE

Pour over tortellini or other pasta.

Whipping cream	**1 cup**	**250 mL**
Butter or hard margarine	**1 tbsp.**	**15 mL**
Grated Parmesan cheese	**²⁄₃ cup**	**150 mL**
Chopped fresh parsley	**¹⁄₄ cup**	**60 mL**
Salt	**¹⁄₈ tsp.**	**0.5 mL**

Mix all 5 ingredients in saucepan. Bring to a slow simmer. Makes 1²⁄₃ cups (400 mL).

Pictured below.

Nothing improves a dish like a delicious tomato-based sauce! These well-seasoned recipes are perfect for pasta, pizza, meatballs, fish or poultry. Save yourself time by doubling or tripling these recipes and freeze for future use.

SPAGHETTI SAUCE

Serve over pasta. For a variation, cook meatballs in sauce as it simmers.

Chopped onion	1 cup	250 mL
Canned tomatoes, with juice, mashed	28 oz.	796 mL
Tomato paste	5½ oz.	156 mL
Canned sliced mushrooms, drained	10 oz.	284 mL
Granulated sugar	2 tsp.	10 mL
Parsley flakes	1 tsp.	5 mL
Salt	1 tsp.	5 mL
Pepper	¼ tsp.	1 mL
Bay leaf	1	1

Measure all 9 ingredients into large saucepan. Mix. Stir occasionally as sauce simmers, uncovered, for 20 minutes. Cover and simmer 20 to 25 minutes more. Discard bay leaf. Makes 4½ cups (1.1 L).

SPAGHETTI SAUCE

Meaty version. While usually served over spaghetti, it is equally good over potatoes or rice.

Ground beef	**1½ lbs.**	**680 g**
Envelope spaghetti sauce mix	1 × 1½ oz.	1 × 42 g
Tomato paste	5½ oz.	156 mL
Canned mushroom pieces, with liquid	10 oz.	284 mL
Canned tomatoes, with juice	19 oz.	540 mL
Medium onion, sliced	1	1
Garlic salt	¼ tsp.	1 mL
Salt	½ tsp.	2 mL
Pepper	¼ tsp.	1 mL

Scramble-fry beef in frying pan until brown. Transfer to large saucepan.

Add remaining ingredients to saucepan. Stir. Bring to a boil. Simmer about 1 hour. Makes 4 cups (1 L).

Pictured below.

TIP

Freeze ripe, unpeeled tomatoes in bags of about 5 (equal to about 14 oz., 398 mL can). When making tomato sauce, simply defrost, break up and remove skin. Tomatoes will be mushy and just right for any of these recipes.

Top: Marinara Sauce, page 64. Bottom: Chicken Sauce, page 60.

CHICKEN SAUCE

Serve over pasta noodles or use in your favorite lasagne recipe instead of the meat sauce.

Butter or hard margarine	2 tbsp.	30 mL
Finely chopped onion	1 cup	250 mL
Ground raw chicken (or chopped cooked chicken)	1¼ lbs.	560 g
Condensed chicken broth	10 oz.	284 mL
Canned sliced mushrooms, drained	10 oz.	284 mL
Canned tomatoes, with juice, broken up	14 oz.	398 mL
Tomato paste	5½ oz.	156 mL
Dried sweet basil	1 tsp.	5 mL
Garlic powder	¼ tsp.	1 mL
Whole oregano	½ tsp.	2 mL
Salt	¾ tsp.	4 mL
Pepper	¼ tsp.	1 mL

Melt butter in large saucepan. Add onion and chicken. Scramble-fry until browned.

Add remaining ingredients. Stir. Bring to a boil. Simmer, uncovered, for about 20 minutes. Makes 6 cups (1.5 L).

Pictured on page 61.

PARÉ
pointer

Little Tommy had to

quit tap-dancing. He

kept falling in the

sink.

TOMATO SAUCE

Ready for pasta or meatloaf.

Tomato sauce	2 × 7½ oz.	2 × 213 mL
Finely chopped onion	1½ cups	375 mL
Whole oregano	½ tsp.	2 mL
Parsley flakes	½ tsp.	2 mL
Garlic powder	¼ tsp.	1 mL

Put all 5 ingredients into saucepan. Bring to a boil, stirring often. Simmer, uncovered, for about 20 minutes until thickened. Makes 2 cups (500 mL).

TOMATO SAUCE

This is the sauce to make when it is more convenient to use canned tomatoes rather than fresh. Makes a good all-round sauce.

Cooking oil	2 tbsp.	30 mL
Finely chopped onion	1½ cups	375 mL
Garlic clove, minced	1	1
Canned tomatoes, with juice, mashed	2 × 19 oz.	2 × 540 mL
Tomato sauce	7½ oz.	213 mL
Parsley flakes	1 tbsp.	15 mL
Granulated sugar	1 tbsp.	15 mL
Salt	1½ tsp.	7 mL
Seasoned salt	1½ tsp.	7 mL
Pepper	¼ tsp.	1 mL
Whole oregano	1 tsp.	5 mL
Dried sweet basil	1 tsp.	5 mL

Heat cooking oil in Dutch oven over medium heat. Add onion and garlic. Sauté about 5 minutes until soft.

Add remaining ingredients. Stir. Bring to a boil. Boil, uncovered, for about 1 hour, stirring occasionally, until desired consistency. Makes about 4 cups (1 L).

PARÉ
pointer

Rivers become

crooked by following

the line of least

resistance. So do

some people.

PIZZA SAUCE

Makes enough for 2 large pizzas. Freeze any extra.

Butter or hard margarine	1 tbsp.	15 mL
Small onion, coarsely chopped	1	1
Canned tomatoes, with juice	19 oz.	540 mL
Bay leaf	1	1
Granulated sugar	1 tsp.	5 mL
Ground oregano	½ tsp.	2 mL
Salt	1 tsp.	5 mL
Pepper, light sprinkle		

Heat butter in large saucepan. Add onion. Sauté until soft.

Add tomatoes, bay leaf, sugar, oregano, salt and pepper. Bring to a boil. Cover. Cook slowly for about 30 minutes, stirring occasionally, until sauce has thickened slightly. Discard bay leaf. Remove from heat. Makes 2¼ cups (560 mL).

MEAT SAUCE

A bit different with the addition of carrot.

Ground beef	½ lb.	225 g
Grated carrot	½ cup	125 mL
Chopped onion	½ cup	125 mL
Olive oil, or cooking oil	2 tbsp.	30 mL
Canned tomatoes, with juice, chopped	19 oz.	540 mL
Granulated sugar	1 tsp.	5 mL
Ground oregano	½ tsp.	2 mL
Dried sweet basil	½ tsp.	2 mL
Salt	1 tsp.	5 mL

Scramble fry ground beef, carrot and onion in olive oil in saucepan or frying pan until no pink remains in meat.

Add next 5 ingredients. Bring to a boil. Simmer 30 minutes, uncovered, until thickened. Stir often. Makes 2½ cups (675 mL).

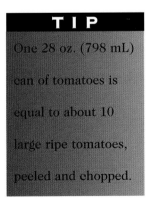

TIP

One 28 oz. (798 mL) can of tomatoes is equal to about 10 large ripe tomatoes, peeled and chopped.

MEXICAN HOT SAUCE

For an authentic taste you will want to add more dried red chilies.
Great with pork or chicken.

Medium tomatoes, peeled and diced	3	3
Finely chopped onion	1/3 cup	75 mL
Chopped chives	1 tbsp.	15 mL
Parsley flakes	1 tsp.	5 mL
Crushed dried red chilies or red pepper flakes	1/2 tsp.	2 mL
Granulated sugar	1/4 tsp.	1 mL
Salt, light sprinkle		

Measure all 7 ingredients into bowl. Stir to mix. Make at least 30 minutes before serving so flavors can blend. Makes about 1 cup (250 mL).

Pictured on this page.

MARINARA SAUCE

One of the well-known pasta sauces. Red and spicy.

Olive oil (or cooking oil)	2 tbsp.	30 mL
Chopped onion	1 cup	250 mL
Garlic cloves, minced	2-3	2-3
Canned tomatoes, with juice, broken up	28 oz.	796 mL
Tomato paste	5 1/2 oz.	156 mL
Granulated sugar	1 tbsp.	15 mL
Parsley flakes	2 tsp.	10 mL
Dried sweet basil	1 1/2 tsp.	7 mL
Ground oregano	1/2 tsp.	2 mL
Salt	1/2 tsp.	2 mL

Heat olive oil in frying pan. Add onion and garlic. Sauté about 5 minutes until soft.

Add tomatoes, tomato paste, sugar, parsley flakes, basil, oregano and salt. Mix well. Bring to a boil. Simmer, uncovered, for about 15 minutes, stirring occasionally. Makes about 2 2/3 cups (650 mL).

Pictured on page 61.

With their distinctive flavor, red and white wines make an excellent ingredient when cooking, particularly in sauces! There is no set rule for choosing your wine except to select one you like. A drier wine may be preferred. Apple juice or white grape juice makes a good substitution for white wine, and all wine can be replaced with alcohol-free wine.

MARSALA WINE SAUCE

Works well with either chicken or veal.

Marsala wine or sherry (or alcohol-free sherry)	3 tbsp.	50 mL
White wine (or alcohol-free white wine)	3 tbsp.	50 mL
Water	1 cup	250 mL
Chicken bouillon powder	1 tbsp.	15 mL
Cornstarch	2 tbsp.	30 mL

Measure all 5 ingredients into small saucepan. Mix well. Stir over medium heat until sauce boils and thickens. Makes 1 cup (250 mL).

RED WINE SAUCE

Spoon over tenderloin fillets.

Water	1 cup	250 mL
Beef bouillon powder	2 tsp.	10 mL
Tomato sauce	2 tbsp.	30 mL
Red wine (or alcohol-free red wine)	1/4 cup	60 mL
Paprika	1 tbsp.	15 mL
Ground savory	1/8 tsp.	0.5 mL
Onion salt	1/2 tsp.	2 mL
Garlic powder	1/8 tsp.	0.5 mL

Combine all 8 ingredients in frying pan. Stir as you bring mixture to a boil. Makes 1 1/3 cups (325 mL).

BÉARNAISE SAUCE

Excellent with seafood or steak.

White wine (or alcohol-free white wine)	2 tbsp.	30 mL
Tarragon vinegar	1 tbsp.	15 mL
Chopped green onion	1 tbsp.	15 mL
Dried tarragon	1 tsp.	5 mL
Pepper	¼ tsp.	1 mL
Egg yolks (large)	3	3
Butter (not margarine), melted	½ cup	125 mL

Bring wine, vinegar, green onion, tarragon and pepper to a boil in small saucepan. Remove from heat. Cover.

Put egg yolks into blender. Blend together. With blender running add butter very slowly in a thin stream. Add tarragon mixture. Blend 6 seconds. Keep hot over hot water. If sauce curdles, whisk in 1 to 2 tbsp. (15 to 30 mL) water. Makes 1 cup (250 mL).

Pictured below.

CHERRY SAUCE

Spoon over baked chicken breasts or ham slices.

Butter or hard margarine	3 tbsp.	50 mL
Chopped onion	1 cup	250 mL
Garlic clove, minced	1	1
Chopped celery	½ cup	125 mL
Grated carrot	1 cup	250 mL
All-purpose flour	¼ cup	60 mL
Salt	1 tsp.	5 mL
Pepper	¼ tsp.	1 mL
Ground cloves, pinch		
Beef bouillon powder	2 tsp.	10 mL
Water	1 cup	250 mL
Red wine (or alcohol-free red wine)	¼ cup	60 mL
Canned pitted cherries, with juice, halved	14 oz.	398 mL

Melt butter in frying pan. Add onion, garlic, celery and carrot. Sauté until soft.

Mix in flour, salt, pepper, cloves and bouillon powder. Add water and wine. Stir until mixture boils and thickens. Add cherries and juice. Return to a boil. Makes 3½ cups (875 mL).

Pictured on this page.

Mushroom Sauce, page 69

MUSHROOM SAUCE

Serve over salmon loaf or cooked fresh asparagus.

Butter or hard margarine	3 tbsp.	50 mL
Sliced fresh mushrooms	1 cup	250 mL
All-purpose flour	2 tbsp.	30 mL
Salt	½ tsp.	2 mL
Pepper	⅛ tsp.	0.5 mL
Paprika	½ tsp.	2 mL
Chicken bouillon powder	½ tsp.	2 mL
Milk	1 cup	250 mL
White wine (or alcohol-free white wine)	1 tbsp.	15 mL

Melt butter in frying pan. Add mushrooms. Sauté until soft.

Sprinkle with flour, salt, pepper, paprika and bouillon powder. Mix well.
Stir in milk and wine until sauce boils and thickens. Makes 1 cup (250 mL).

Pictured on page 68.

WINE SAUCE

Divide this sauce over veal cutlets.

Butter or hard margarine	¼ cup	60 mL
All-purpose flour	¼ cup	60 mL
Salt	½ tsp.	2 mL
Pepper	1/16 tsp.	0.5 mL
Beef bouillon powder	1 tbsp.	15 mL
Milk	2 cups	500 mL
White wine (or alcohol-free white wine)	¼ cup	60 mL

Melt butter in frying pan. Mix in flour, salt, pepper and bouillon powder.
Stir in milk and wine until sauce boils and thickens. Makes 2⅓ cups
(575 mL).

Thinner in consistency than most sauces, marinades are commonly used for soaking beef, pork, poultry, fish or seafood prior to cooking, but this is also a great way to place distinctive flavors directly into your food. Acidic ingredients such as wine, lemon juice or vinegar help tenderize the meat, which then allows the marinade to penetrate. Fish and seafood only require marinating for 30 to 60 minutes. If marinated too long fish will begin to "cook".

FAST TERIYAKI

Double recipe and freeze extra. Keep on hand for quick chicken or steak.

Soy sauce	½ cup	125 mL
Cooking oil	¼ cup	60 mL
Ketchup	1 tbsp.	15 mL
Garlic powder	¼ tsp.	1 mL

Mix soy sauce, cooking oil, ketchup and garlic powder in small bowl. Makes ¾ cup (175 mL).

TIP

To thicken 1 cup (250 mL) marinade, mix 1 tbsp. (15 mL) cornstarch with 2 tbsp. (30 mL) cold water. Pour slowly into boiling marinade, stirring constantly.

TERIYAKI MARINADE

A flavorful marinade for an economy cut of steak.

Soy sauce	⅔ cup	150 mL
Brown sugar, packed	½ cup	125 mL
Sherry (or alcohol-free sherry)	¼ cup	60 mL
Cooking oil	2 tbsp.	30 mL
Ground ginger	1 tsp.	5 mL
Garlic clove, minced	1	1
Seasoned salt	½ tsp.	2 mL

Combine all 7 ingredients in deep bowl. Stir well. Makes 1¼ cups (300 mL).

FAVORITE MARINADE

You can't go wrong with this marinade. Boil and thicken any remaining marinade with 1 tbsp. (15 mL) cornstarch mixed with 2 tbsp. (30 mL) water and use as sauce.

Soy sauce	½ cup	125 mL
Sherry (or use red wine vinegar)	½ cup	125 mL
White vinegar	3 tbsp.	50 mL
Cooking oil	2 tbsp.	30 mL
Granulated sugar	2 tbsp.	30 mL
Ground ginger	½ tsp.	2 mL
Garlic powder	¼ tsp.	1 mL
Pepper	¼ tsp.	1 mL

Combine all 8 ingredients in small bowl. Stir well. Makes 1¼ cups (300 mL).

Pictured on this page.

PIQUANT MARINADE

As the name says, this has a pungent, sharp taste—just right for steak.

Red wine vinegar	½ cup	125 mL
Soy sauce	¼ cup	60 mL
Garlic clove, minced	1	1
Worcestershire sauce	2 tbsp.	30 mL
Prepared mustard	2 tbsp.	30 mL
Cooking oil	½ cup	125 mL

Combine all 6 ingredients in bowl. Stir. Makes 1⅓ cups (325 mL).

CHILI MARINADE

Very light tomato in the marinade. Use with fish.

White vinegar	½ cup	125 mL
Chili sauce	2 tbsp.	30 mL
Cooking oil	2 tbsp.	30 mL
Brown sugar, packed	2 tbsp.	30 mL
Worcestershire sauce	1 tsp.	5 mL
Onion powder	¼ tsp.	1 mL
Garlic powder	¼ tsp.	1 mL
Chili powder	¼ tsp.	1 mL

Combine all 8 ingredients in shallow pan. Makes ⅞ cup (220 mL).

Pictured on this page.

GINGER MARINADE

A tantalizing flavor for stir-fry beef and vegetables.

Soy sauce	3 tbsp.	50 mL
Oyster sauce	2 tbsp.	30 mL
Finely chopped ginger	1½ tbsp.	25 mL
Sherry (or alcohol-free sherry)	2 tbsp.	30 mL
Cornstarch	1 tbsp.	15 mL
Granulated sugar	1 tsp.	5 mL
Salt	½ tsp.	2 mL

Combine all 7 ingredients in deep bowl. Stir well. Makes 6 tbsp. (100 mL).

Pictured on page 75.

LEMON MARINADE

A nice mild marinade for shrimp.

Cooking oil	½ **cup**	125 mL
Juice of 1 small lemon		
Peel of 1 lemon, sliced		
Garlic powder	¼ **tsp.**	1 mL
Salt	¼ **tsp.**	1 mL
Dried thyme	½ **tsp.**	2 mL
Seasoned salt	¼ **tsp.**	1 mL
Pepper, light sprinkle		
Hot pepper sauce (optional)	⅛ **tsp.**	0.5 mL

Mix all 9 ingredients in deep bowl. Makes ¾ cup (175 mL).

Pictured on page 75.

LEMONY DILL SAUCE

Perfect sauce for marinating pork chops.

Salad dressing (or mayonnaise)	6 **tbsp.**	100 mL
Dijon mustard	¼ **cup**	60 mL
Lemon juice, fresh or bottled	¼ **cup**	60 mL
Dill weed	1 **tsp.**	5 mL

Mix all 4 ingredients in small bowl. Makes ⅞ cup (220 mL).

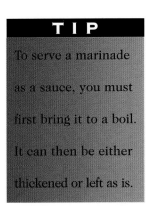

TIP

To serve a marinade as a sauce, you must first bring it to a boil. It can then be either thickened or left as is.

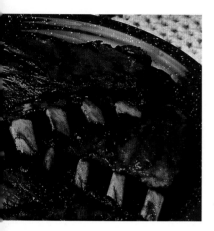

JAVA MARINADE

Different from the usual. Use with pork ribs.

Strong prepared coffee	**1¼ cups**	**300 mL**
Ketchup	**1¼ cups**	**300 mL**
Brown sugar, packed	**⅔ cup**	**150 mL**
Cider vinegar	**½ cup**	**125 mL**
Worcestershire sauce	**4 tsp.**	**20 mL**

Measure all 5 ingredients into large bowl. Stir to dissolve sugar. Makes 3¼ cups (800 mL).

Pictured on this page.

TOMATO MARINADE

Wonderful for ribs.

Tomato sauce	**7½ oz.**	**213 mL**
Cider vinegar	**½ cup**	**125 mL**
Dry onion flakes	**1 tbsp.**	**15 mL**
Worcestershire sauce	**2 tsp.**	**10 mL**
Granulated sugar	**1½ tbsp.**	**25 mL**
Prepared mustard	**1 tsp.**	**5 mL**
Pepper	**½ tsp.**	**2 mL**
Chili powder	**1 tsp.**	**5 mL**
Garlic powder	**¼ tsp.**	**1 mL**
Cooking oil	**¼ cup**	**60 mL**

Combine all 10 ingredients in small bowl. Stir well. Makes 1½ cups (375 mL).

Pictured on page 75.

*Clockwise from top left: Tomato Marinade, page 74;
Ginger Marinade, page 72; and Lemon Marinade, page 73.*

MAUI SAUCE

After using this pineapple sauce for a marinade, boil and use as a sauce.

Canned crushed pineapple, with juice	**19 oz.**	**540 mL**
Soy sauce	**½ cup**	**125 mL**
Granulated sugar	**2 tbsp.**	**30 mL**
Ground ginger	**½ tsp.**	**2 mL**
Garlic powder	**½ tsp.**	**2 mL**
Pepper	**¼ tsp.**	**1 mL**

Put all 6 ingredients into bowl. Stir. Makes 2¾ cups (675 mL).

Pictured on this page.

ONION SOUP MARINADE

Great for kabobs.

Sherry (or alcohol-free sherry)	**½ cup**	**125 mL**
Soy sauce	**½ cup**	**125 mL**
Lemon juice, fresh or bottled	**1 tbsp.**	**15 mL**
Envelope dry onion soup mix	**1 × 1½ oz.**	**1 × 42 g**
Brown sugar, packed	**2 tbsp.**	**30 mL**
Cooking oil	**2 tbsp.**	**30 mL**

Combine sherry, soy sauce, lemon juice, onion soup mix, brown sugar and cooking oil in deep bowl. Mix well. Makes 1¼ cups (300 mL).

PARÉ
pointer

A good magician is a

super-duper.

Measurement Tables

Throughout this book measurements are given in Conventional and Metric measure. To compensate for differences between the two measurements due to rounding, a full metric measure is not always used. The cup used is the standard 8 fluid ounce. Temperature is given in degrees Fahrenheit and Celsius. Baking pan measurements are in inches and centimetres as well as quarts and litres. An exact metric conversion is given below as well as the working equivalent (Standard Measure).

OVEN TEMPERATURES

Fahrenheit (°F)	Celsius (°C)
175°	80°
200°	95°
225°	110°
250°	120°
275°	140°
300°	150°
325°	160°
350°	175°
375°	190°
400°	205°
425°	220°
450°	230°
475°	240°
500°	260°

SPOONS

Conventional Measure	Metric Exact Conversion Millilitre (mL)	Metric Standard Measure Millilitre (mL)
1/8 teaspoon (tsp.)	0.6 mL	0.5 mL
1/4 teaspoon (tsp.)	1.2 mL	1 mL
1/2 teaspoon (tsp.)	2.4 mL	2 mL
1 teaspoon (tsp.)	4.7 mL	5 mL
2 teaspoons (tsp.)	9.4 mL	10 mL
1 tablespoon (tbsp.)	14.2 mL	15 mL

CUPS

Conventional Measure	Metric Exact Conversion Millilitre (mL)	Metric Standard Measure Millilitre (mL)
1/4 cup (4 tbsp.)	56.8 mL	50 mL
1/3 cup (5 1/3 tbsp.)	75.6 mL	75 mL
1/2 cup (8 tbsp.)	113.7 mL	125 mL
2/3 cup (10 2/3 tbsp.)	151.2 mL	150 mL
3/4 cup (12 tbsp.)	170.5 mL	175 mL
1 cup (16 tbsp.)	227.3 mL	250 mL
4 1/2 cups	1022.9 mL	1000 mL (1 L)

PANS

Conventional Inches	Metric Centimetres
8x8 inch	20x20 cm
9x9 inch	22x22 cm
9x13 inch	22x33 cm
10x15 inch	25x38 cm
11x17 inch	28x43 cm
8x2 inch round	20x5 cm
9x2 inch round	22x5 cm
10x4 1/2 inch tube	25x11 cm
8x4x3 inch loaf	20x10x7 cm
9x5x3 inch loaf	22x12x7 cm

DRY MEASUREMENTS

Conventional Measure Ounces (oz.)	Metric Exact Conversion Grams (g)	Metric Standard Measure Grams (g)
1 oz.	28.3 g	30 g
2 oz.	56.7 g	55 g
3 oz.	85.0 g	85 g
4 oz.	113.4 g	125 g
5 oz.	141.7 g	140 g
6 oz.	170.1 g	170 g
7 oz.	198.4 g	200 g
8 oz.	226.8 g	250 g
16 oz.	453.6 g	500 g
32 oz.	907.2 g	1000 g (1 KG)

CASSEROLES (CANADA & BRITAIN)

Standard Size Casserole	Exact Metric Measure
1 qt. (5 cups)	1.13 L
1 1/2 qts. (7 1/2 cups)	1.69 L
2 qts. (10 cups)	2.25 L
2 1/2 qts. (12 1/2 cups)	2.81 L
3 qts. (15 cups)	3.38 L
4 qts. (20 cups)	4.5 L
5 qts. (25 cups)	5.63 L

CASSEROLES (UNITED STATES)

Standard Size Casserole	Exact Metric Measure
1 qt. (4 cups)	900 mL
1 1/2 qts. (6 cups)	1.35 L
2 qts. (8 cups)	1.8 L
2 1/2 qts. (10 cups)	2.25 L
3 qts. (12 cups)	2.7 L
4 qts. (16 cups)	3.6 L
5 qts. (20 cups)	4.5 L

Index

COOKBOOKS

Teriyaki Sauce, page 6

Creating everyday recipes you can trust!

Company's Coming cookbooks are available at retail locations everywhere.

For information contact:

COMPANY'S COMING PUBLISHING LIMITED

Box 8037, Station "F"
Edmonton, Alberta
Canada T6H 4N9

Box 17870
San Diego, California
U.S.A. 92177-7870

TEL: (403) 450-6223
FAX: (403) 450-1857